14.00

Accelerated **R**eade**R**
LEVEL   POINTS
8.2   1.0

D1570150

Eyes on the Sky

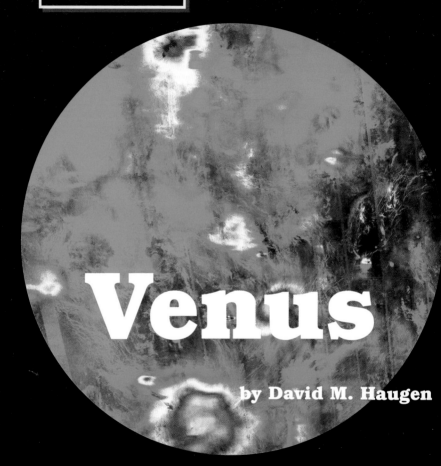

Venus

by David M. Haugen

KidHaven Press

KidHaven Press, an imprint of Gale Group, Inc.,
10911 Technology Place, San Diego, CA 92127

Library of Congress Cataloging-in-Publication Data

Haugen, David M., 1969–
    Venus/by David M. Haugen.
        p. cm. — (Eyes on the sky)
    Includes bibliographical references and index.
    ISBN 0-7377-0940-5 (lib. bdg. : alk. paper)
    1. Venus (Planet)—Juvenile literature. [1. Venus (Planet)]
    I. Title. II. Our solar system (San Diego, Calif.)
    QB621 .H38 2002
    523.42—dc21

2001000853

Copyright 2002 by KidHaven Press, an imprint of Gale Group, Inc., 10911 Technology Place, San Diego, CA 92127

Printed in the U.S.A.

Table of Contents

1
A Place in the Solar System

The planet Venus appears to shine like a star in the night sky. For centuries people have referred to Venus as the Evening Star or the Morning Star because, other than the sun and the moon, it is the brightest heavenly body visible from Earth. Although Venus is not a star, its glowing appearance has captivated stargazers since ancient times. The early Romans were so taken with Venus that they named the planet after their goddess of beauty and love.

Venus seems so large and bright in the nighttime sky because it is the planet that passes closest to Earth. When the two planets are nearest each other, they are separated by only 26.1 million miles. This may seem like a long distance, but Earth's other neighbor, the planet Mars, is 35 million miles away at its closest approach. Both Venus and Mars, however, are close enough to be seen with the naked eye from Earth.

Venus's Orbit and Rotation

Venus, Earth, and Mars are the second, third, and fourth planets from the sun, the center of the solar system. Each of these planets, as well as the six other planets in the solar system, circle—or **orbit**—around the sun at varying distances. Venus traces its orbit at about 67 million miles from the sun. This is about three-quarters of the distance from Earth to the sun.

While making its orbit, Venus moves through space rather rapidly. Earth takes 365 days to make one solar orbit, but Venus travels much faster. It completes its orbit in only 225 Earth days. Each planet in the solar system circles the sun at its own pace. This is why Venus and Earth are not always 26.1 million miles apart. At certain times in their unequal orbits, Venus is on the opposite side of the sun from Earth and appears slightly smaller in the night sky.

As it travels through space, Venus—like all planets—rotates. Earth rotates once in

The Nine Planets

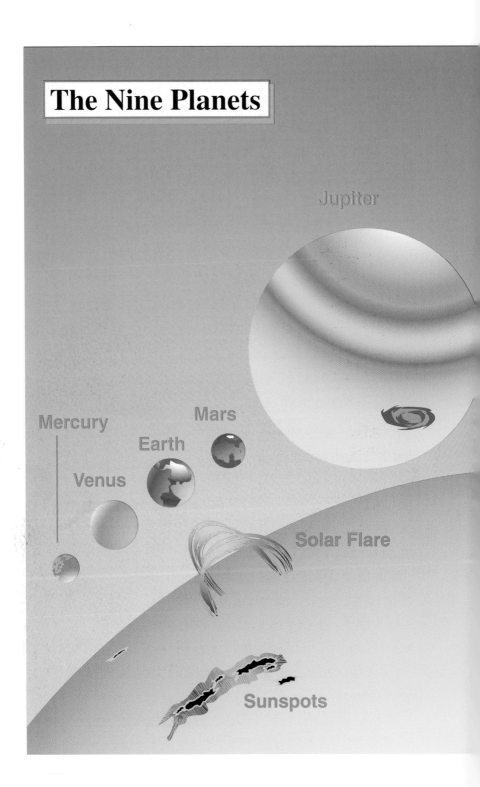

Jupiter

Mercury

Mars

Earth

Venus

Solar Flare

Sunspots

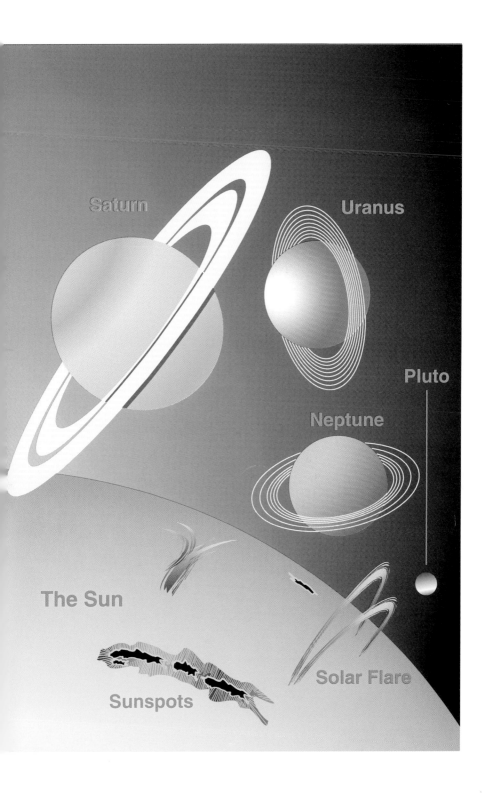

Saturn

Uranus

Pluto

Neptune

The Sun

Solar Flare

Sunspots

twenty-four hours, completing an Earth day. Venus, however, rotates very slowly. It spins on its axis once in 243 Earth days. Since a year on Venus is only 225 days (the time it takes to go around the sun once), it takes more than one year for the planet to make a complete rotation.

Venus's rotation is also unusual because the planet has **retrograde motion**—that is, it spins from east to west. Most other planets in the solar system rotate in the opposite direction. Only Venus and distant Pluto have retrograde motion, so from their surfaces, the sun appears to rise in the west and set in the east.

The Phases of Venus

As Venus traces its circular path around the sun, it appears to change shape and size when viewed from Earth. Similar to Earth's moon, Venus has phases. During its phases, the planet will transform from a full circle, to a half circle, to a slim crescent, and eventually back to a full circle again. Just as with the moon, the phases of Venus are determined by how earthbound observers view the sunlight striking the planet. Venus reflects sunlight so well, however, that even as a slim crescent, the planet appears very bright in Earth's sky.

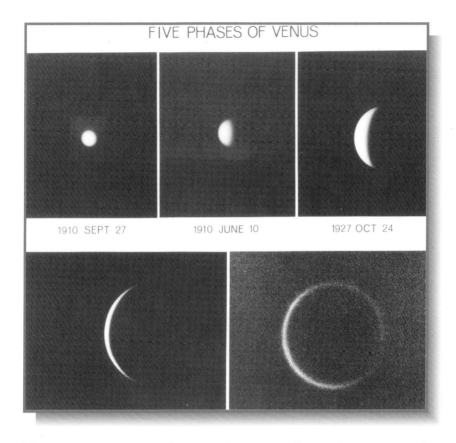

FIVE PHASES OF VENUS

1910 SEPT 27   1910 JUNE 10   1927 OCT 24

Venus appears to change shape as it revolves around the sun, much as the moon does.

During its phases, Venus appears to shrink as it moves farther away from Earth. From this basic observation, a seventeenth-century Italian astronomer named Galileo Galilei drew important conclusions about the organization of the solar system. Using one of the first telescopes, Galileo watched Venus pass through its phases and noticed the planet appeared to be smaller when it was a full circle than when it was a slim crescent.

Evidence of a Sun-Centered Solar System

To Galileo, the changing size of Venus confirmed his belief in a theory presented by a Polish monk named Nicolaus Copernicus. Through his own observations, Copernicus believed the sun was the center of the solar system and the planets traced paths around it. Although this concept is taken for granted today, in the times of Copernicus and Galileo, most people believed strongly that Earth was the center of the universe and that all heavenly bodies rotated around it.

The fact that Venus changed size proved to Galileo that Copernicus's theory was more accurate than the traditional beliefs. When Venus is on the far side of the sun, it appears as a small but bright disc because the illuminated side of the planet is visible from Earth. When Venus moves in between the sun and Earth, however, the planet appears as a large sliver of light. Although Venus is closer to Earth in this instance, its illuminated side is now facing away from Earth, and only a few of the sun's rays are able to edge around the rim of the planet to reach Earth. To explain these observations, Galileo rightly concluded that Venus had to be orbiting the sun and not Earth.

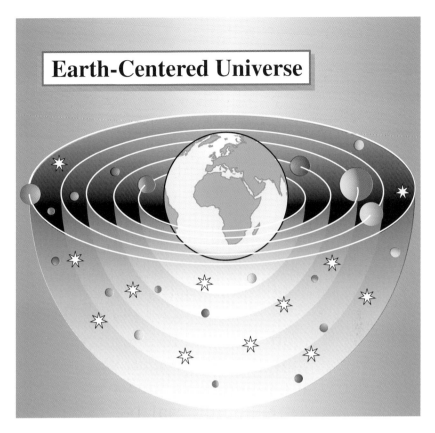

Earth-Centered Universe

At the time of Copernicus and Galileo it was widely believed that Earth was the center of the universe.

Galileo was pleased with his discovery, but he knew many authorities would not be. The Catholic Church, for example, condemned the belief in a sun-centered solar system. Eventually Galileo was brought before the church's court and forced to deny Copernicus's theory and pledge anew his belief in the church's doctrine of an Earth-centered universe. With the continuing dominance of religious power in Europe, it was many years

Venus's crescent is easy to see in the evening sky.

The Catholic Church forced Galileo to refute the theory of a sun-centered solar system.

before Copernicus's theory was generally acknowledged to be true.

The Shining Mystery

Observing Venus's phases helped prove that the sun was at the center of the solar system. It was a great discovery that forever changed scientific thinking—especially in the field of astronomy. Yet for having played such an important part in changing the way people viewed their position in the universe, Venus remained a relatively uncharted planet. Even with advancements in telescopes, the shiny white surface of the Evening Star revealed nothing to observers. For three centuries astronomers could only guess what the surface of Venus was like and whether life might exist on the distant planet.

2

Earth's Twin

Because Venus was Earth's closest neighbor, astronomers from the seventeenth century onward turned their telescopes on the planet in hopes of finding something useful to study. The earliest of these scientists found little, however. Venus appeared as a pale white ball that seemed to have no special markings. As telescopes improved, astronomers realized the whiteness they saw was a cloud layer that covered the planet. Although these scientists wished to know more about what lay below the white covering, Venus's clouds kept the interior of the planet a mystery.

Obvious Similarities

Faced with such an obstacle, astronomers gathered what information they could from

Venus has a thick cloud layer that gives it a pale white appearance.

their observations. Almost immediately scientists measured the size of Venus, noting that the planet's **diameter**—or the distance across its center—was 7,523 miles. This meant that Venus was just slightly smaller than Earth. Coupled with the fact that the two planets were so close together in the solar system, many astronomers believed that Venus was Earth's twin. With this idea guiding their research, astronomers right up to the nineteenth century began noticing—or imagining—other similarities between the planets.

Some astronomers thought they spotted features within the cloud formations, and they tracked these markings as they traveled across the visible surface. From this data these scientists mistakenly determined that the planet rotated in a period close to twenty-

Venus (left) and Earth are similar in size and distance from the sun, which led some astronomers to refer to them as twin planets.

four hours, just like Earth does. Others who trained their telescopes on the planet believed they saw continents and oceans appear in gaps in the cloud cover. These sightings seemed to support the theory that Earth and Venus might be twin planets.

As science improved in the eighteenth and nineteenth centuries, scientists saw even more similarities between the two planets. Astronomers discovered the mass of Venus to be just over 82 percent of Earth's mass. Likewise, its surface **gravity** was 91 percent of that on Earth. With such revealing measurements, the theory of Earth's twin gained in popularity among scientists. Some believed the two planets were so similar that the possibility of life on Venus was strong.

Early Hopes for Life on Venus

Among the earliest scientists to note "evidence" of life on Venus was the German astronomer Franz von Paula Gruithuisen. At the close of the 1800s, von Paula Gruithuisen saw a glimmer of light on a darkened rim of the planet. Having no other explanation for the sighting, he guessed the light was from huge celebrations to honor new rulers of Venus. Later von Paula Gruithuisen offered a different explanation for the light. He claimed the

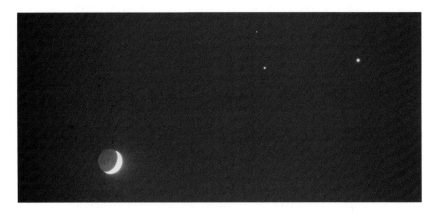

German astronomer Franz von Paula Gruithuisen believed that the sliver of light on Venus was from a huge celebration on the planet.

glow came from the seasonal fires Venusians supposedly lit to clear land for planting crops.

Although von Paula Gruithuisen's claims could not be supported by facts, other theories about life on Venus were based on common observation. Seeing only Venus's white mask, for example, scientists had to guess about what kind of atmosphere and surface conditions could exist under such heavy cloud cover.

In 1918 Swedish chemist Svante Arrhenius thought Venus must have a humid atmosphere. Thinking of places on Earth that are very humid, Arrhenius assumed that Venus was probably covered in swamplands. The moisture, he predicted, would cover the primitive plant life. Arrhenius believed similar swamps covered Earth in its infancy. Therefore, he concluded that Venus, like Earth, might develop more advanced plant and animal life, perhaps soon enough to take over when life on Earth became extinct.

Other scientists in later years put forth different notions of what might exist under the cloud layers. In the 1920s a group of American scientists thought the clouds would keep temperatures on Venus so hot that the landscape would be one vast, dry desert. In the early 1950s a British scientist named Fred Hoyle proposed that Venus might be covered by a large ocean of oil. Scientists debated these theories and many others like them until new technology gave them new and better information.

Evidence of an Uninhabitable Environment

In 1956 astronomers using new radio telescopes detected radio waves coming from Venus. The specific wave pattern indicated that Venus was a very hot planet. Temperatures recorded through a careful study of the radio waves showed the surface of Venus to be over 750 degrees Fahrenheit. Such a high heat level ruled out many earlier theories about Venus's landscape. There would be very little, if any, water on the hot planet, so plant and animal life could not exist.

Temperatures on Venus can be more than 750 degrees Fahrenheit.

The newly detected radio emissions were not the first bit of evidence to suggest Venus was quite different from Earth. As early as the 1930s, scientists had used **spectroscopes**—instruments that can detect the presence of specific elements by the light they give off—to read what elements were present in Venus's atmosphere. These early readings showed Venus to have a large amount of **carbon dioxide**—a poisonous gas—in its atmosphere. Earthbound spectroscopes, however, can give false readings because they must view the light from other planets as it passes through Earth's atmosphere. The elements in Earth's atmosphere can mar the spectroscopic findings. Because of this potential for error, many astronomers who believed that Venus was Earth's twin chose to ignore the evidence. Only when radio telescopes strengthened the notion that life could not exist on Venus did the scientific community accept that Venus and Earth were different enough to disprove the twin planet theory.

Secrets Yet to Be Revealed

Knowing that the surface of Venus lacked water and plants, astronomers concluded that the planet must be dry and rocky. The radio telescopes, however, told them little more. A greater scientific advancement would be needed to reveal more of Venus's secrets. In less than a decade, that advancement would come in the form of unmanned space missions to the mysterious planet. Several probes would pass by Venus and help astronomers learn far more about Earth's neighbor than earthbound observation ever could reveal.

3
A Deadly Planet

In the 1960s two nations—the United States and the Soviet Union—were determined to explore as much of space and the neighboring planets as they could. Both countries had the technology and the money to create space programs that could fulfill their desire to reach the stars. Early unmanned spacecraft began leaving Earth's atmosphere in the first years of the decade, and one of their first targets was our closest planetary neighbor.

To Reach Venus

In 1961 the Soviet Union had developed a rocket that could send a probe on its way to Venus. Called *Venera 1*, the poorly aimed spacecraft passed too far away from Venus, and since no camera was on board, the probe failed to send back any useful information. *Venera 2*, launched immediately after, came within fifteen thousand miles of Venus, but it suffered equipment failure, leaving the probe unable to send any information about the planet. With these faltering first steps, the Soviets spent time improving their spacecraft. It would be about five years before the Venera program achieved results.

Meanwhile in the United States, the newly created National Aeronautics and Space Administration (NASA) set its sights on reaching

In 1962 the *Mariner 2* spacecraft took readings and recorded information about Venus's atmosphere.

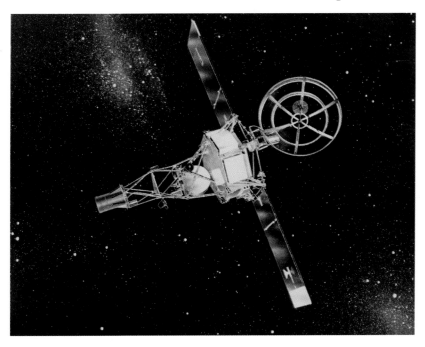

Venus with its own *Mariner 2* spacecraft. Launched in 1962, *Mariner 2* came within 21,750 miles of Venus. The instruments on board took readings of the planet's temperature as well as the types of particles in its atmosphere.

The Greenhouse Planet

With data streaming back to Earth, *Mariner 2* confirmed some of the theories about Venus. The probe recorded temperatures of 900 degrees Fahrenheit at the planet's surface. This is the highest surface temperature of any planet in the solar system. The instruments on *Mariner 2* also found that carbon dioxide made up over 96 percent of the atmosphere. The large amount of carbon dioxide explains the planet's high surface heat.

Venus suffers from what scientists call the **greenhouse effect**. Sunlight streams into Venus's atmosphere, and some of it reaches the surface of the planet. The surface heats up and emits another form of heat back into the atmosphere. However, the carbon dioxide that allows the sun's heat in does not let the surface heat out. The atmosphere heats up like the air inside a greenhouse. Yet a greenhouse has ways of venting some of the heat to keep a stable temperature. Since no surface heat escapes Venus, the temperatures reach levels that are so high, they would melt soft metals like lead and zinc.

Clouds of Acid

The very high temperatures of the planet's atmosphere confirmed the view that life cannot

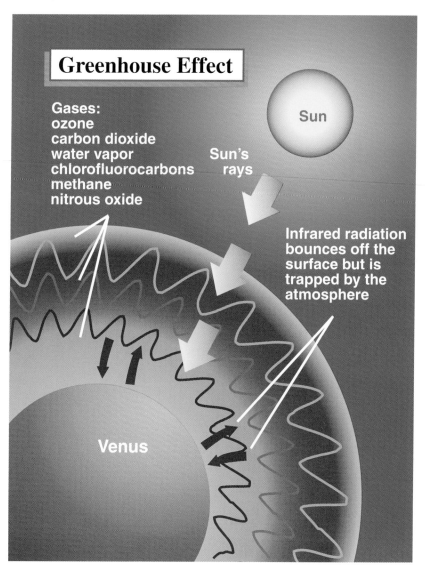

Greenhouse Effect

Gases:
ozone
carbon dioxide
water vapor
chlorofluorocarbons
methane
nitrous oxide

Sun

Sun's rays

Infrared radiation bounces off the surface but is trapped by the atmosphere

Venus

Layers of clouds extend for fifteen miles above Venus.

exist on Venus. *Mariner 2*, however, found evidence that Venus was not only unlivable but deadly. Sensors showed that the cloud layers covering Venus are mostly made up of tiny drops of **sulfuric acid**, a dangerous substance that eats away at anything it touches.

The cloud cover starts about thirty miles from the planet's surface and extends upward for fifteen miles. Within this billowy mass, three layers can be seen. The highest cloud layer contains the most sulfuric acid (nearly 85 percent), while the lower layers have much less. Inside the lowest cloud layer, which extends upward for only two miles, there are also some larger particles. These may be pure sulfur, a yellowish element that probably gives the planet its pale hue.

Measuring the temperatures in these cloud banks, *Mariner 2* recorded a range of numbers. The lowest cloud layers are a scorching 212 degrees Fahrenheit. These temperatures taper off quickly at higher elevations. The very top of the cloud mass registers below freezing at −40 degrees Fahrenheit.

Continuing Missions to Venus

Mariner 2 returned a great deal of useful information about Venus. Over the next few decades, more spacecraft—both American and Russian—would make the trip to Venus. The United States continued its Mariner program, sending probes that passed by the planet on their way to scout out distant Mercury. On its flyby in 1967, *Mariner 5* returned more accurate readings of Venus's size and mass. In 1974, *Mariner 10* sent back video images of the planet. Using infrared technology, these cameras peered through the bright mask of the planet to capture photos of the

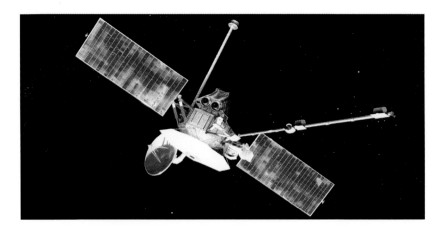

Mariner 10, sent in 1974, used infrared cameras to take photos of Venus's thick clouds.

clouds themselves. It was the Soviet Union, however, that would take greater measures and send spacecraft into Venus itself, sending back the first information about the interior of Venus and its unseen surface.

A High-Pressure Atmosphere

By 1967 the Soviet Union's Venera space program was back on track. In that year *Venera 4* was launched. This newly designed spacecraft sent a round probe into Venus's cloud layers. Equipped with heat-stopping parachutes, the globe descended slowly through the atmosphere, taking readings all the while. The harsh sulfuric atmosphere, however, ate away at the probe, causing its instruments to fail before it reached the planet's surface.

Before it died, *Venera 4* did reveal new information about Venus's atmosphere. Transmitted data indicated that Venus had an atmospheric pressure ninety times greater than that on Earth. Although man-made objects could survive this pressure for some time, the *Venera 4* was not designed for such crushing forces. Certainly no human could stand the pressure either.

Between 1967 and 1982, the Soviets launched ten more Venera probes to Venus. Although each probe was designed to better withstand the harsh atmosphere, some still experienced equipment failures. Several, however, did reach the surface intact. While these only lasted an hour before being flattened by the tremendous surface pressure, the probes did send back useful information that helped scientists learn more about the planet's terrain. In 1975 *Venera 9* sent back the first black-and-white images of a landscape composed of sharp-edged rocks that jutted up toward the sky. *Venera 10*, launched the same year, landed in a flat region of smooth stone. *Venera 13* and *14* brought color cameras to Venus. Arriving in 1982, the two probes—the last of the Venera missions to land on the planet—sent back images of a barren, rocky terrain and a hazy sky, both bathed in a reddish-orange light.

New Probes, New Discoveries

After celebrating the landmark achievements of *Venera 13* and *14*, the Soviet Union sent only two more probes into the interior of Venus. Arriving in 1985, the newly designed *Vega 1* and *Vega 2* had the task of launching weather balloons into Venus's atmosphere while the probes descended to the planet's surface. Scientists all over the world could track the balloons' progress and share in the information the ballons' instruments recorded as they drifted through the atmosphere of Venus.

Despite the successes of many of these missions, the cost of sending expensive probes

Venera 4, sent by the Soviet Union, sent a probe into Venus's cloud layers to take pictures of its surface. The Venera 4 is seen here at right in comparison to a later image taken by *Magellan*.

Orbiters to Venus gathered new information about
Venus's landscape hidden under its thick clouds.

to their doom in the harsh Venus environment
proved too high. Both the Soviet Union and the
United States turned to orbiting probes to
learn more about Venus. These orbiters car-
ried new instruments that allowed astronomers to see below Venus's cloud cover
and map the entire landscape of the planet. Finally, scientists would get a better under-
standing of the unusual geography that lay
hidden from view for so long.

4

The Geography of Venus

While NASA and the Soviet Union were sending space probes to Venus during the late twentieth century, scientific radar stations on Earth were beginning to map parts of the planet's landscape. Huge radar dishes send signals to Venus and "read" them as they bounce off the planet and return to Earth. By judging how long specific signal waves take to return to the radar station, astronomers can construct crude maps of how the terrain on faraway Venus looks. The maps show raised hills and mountains as well as valleys and craters, but they don't reveal much else about the landscape.

The Four Orbiters

The level of detail of the radar maps grew dramatically when both NASA and the Soviet Union put four different probes into orbit around Venus. *Pioneer 12* (also known as the *Pioneer Venus Orbiter*) was launched by the United States in 1978. It was followed in 1983 by two more Venera spacecraft, numbers 15 and 16, from Russia. Finally, NASA launched the *Magellan* orbiter from the space shuttle *Atlantis* in 1989. These probes remained in orbit around the planet for up to fifteen years, and their radar and other mapping devices greatly aided astronomers.

Radar stations on Earth are able to map Venus clearly only when it is closest to Earth.

Scientists used radar stations to map Venus's landscape, which showed hills, mountains, and valleys.

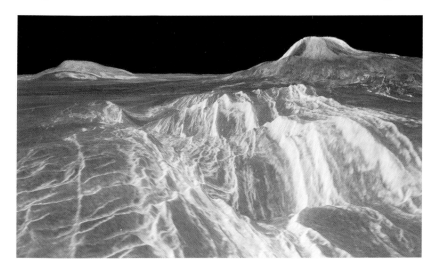

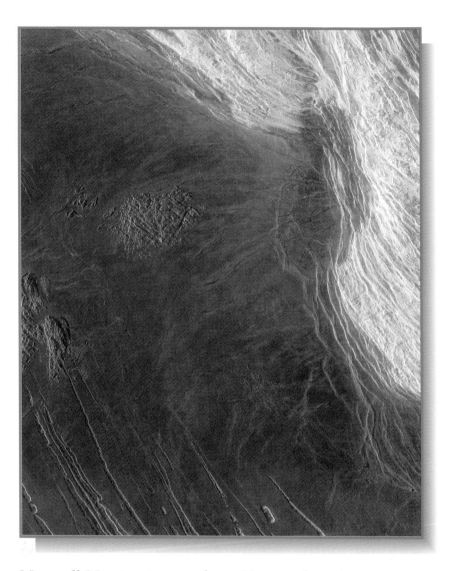

Maxwell Montes is a peak on Venus almost seven miles high.

tain ranges. The most notable of these contains the Maxwell Montes (meaning mountain), a peak that rises nearly seven miles. This is Venus's highest elevation, higher even than Mount Everest, the tallest mountain on Earth.

Volcanic Activity

The third and smallest of the highland regions on Venus is Beta Regio. Its area is mostly taken up by two high mountains, Rhea Mons and Theia Mons. These two peaks are probably extinct volcanoes. Thousands of volcanoes dot the mountain chains found in the highland regions of Venus. Almost all of these volcanoes are considered dead since major eruptions ceased about 500 million years ago. Evidence suggests, however, that some volcanic activity is still taking place on Venus but not on the scale that produced the huge lava flows that cover much of Venus's landscape.

These volcanoes are located in Beta Regio. Most of the volcanoes on Venus are inactive.

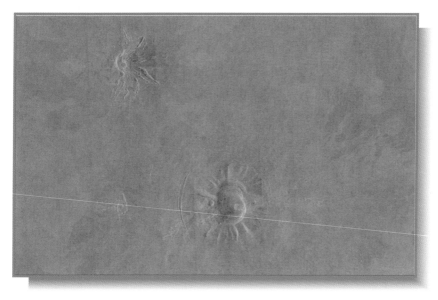

Radar imaging from the *Magellan* probe clearly shows the lava flows that once poured down from active volcanoes and streaked across the land. Some of the smoothest land is actually lava that flattened out as it spread. Other regions show streak patterns where ridges of lava cooled as they snaked over the surface. These features suggest that this lava-scarred surface is new to Venus. The ancient surface would have been covered with impact craters from **asteroids** and **comets** that struck the planet during its early formation. The absence of these craters tells scientists that the lava covered them over as it spread across the land.

Spiderwebs and Pancakes

Amidst the ridges and plains are other markings that also relate to ancient volcanic activity. The *Magellan* probe sent back images of circular ridge patterns that sometimes extended outward for a hundred miles. Called **arachnoids**, because they fan out like webs built by arachnids (the scientific term for spiders), these patterns were probably formed by molten rock just under the surface. The lava pushed upward on the landscape and formed bubbles. When these cooled, they shrank and collapsed in on themselves, leaving a circular network of troughs and ridges.

Other odd features on Venus's surface are the flat-topped hills called **pancake domes**. Their unusual name comes from the fact that from above, these domes look like pancakes cooking on a griddle. Actually they are the ancient site of volcanic activity. Millions of years ago lava close to the planet's surface oozed up out of cracks and formed bubbles. As the lava cooled, it held its domelike shape. The pancake domes sometimes rise as much as twenty-five hundred feet, and their sides are usually very steep. Like the arachnoids, the pancake domes let scientists know that Venus was once a very volcanic planet.

Pancake domes formed from lava rise as much as 25,000 feet with steep sloping sides.

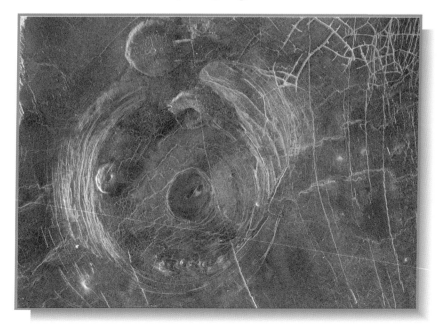

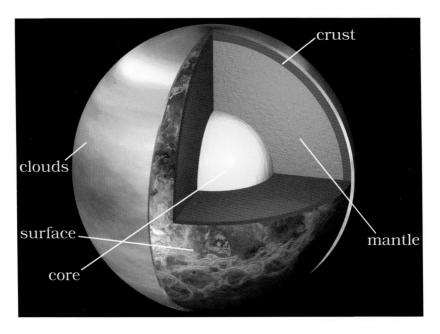

clouds

surface

core

crust

mantle

Venus's surface appears to be a hard shell with a crust twice as thick as Earth's.

A Solid Crust

Although most volcanic activity appears to have ended long ago, astronomers say that the planet must have some way of venting its internal heat. Like Earth, Venus probably has a molten core surrounded by a hard crust that forms the surface. The Earth's surface is made up of many "plates" of land that rest alongside each other like pieces of a jigsaw puzzle. The movement of the plates releases some of the planet's internal energy in the form of earthquakes. Venus's surface, however, does not seem to be a series of plates, and instead appears to be one unbroken shell, perhaps twice as thick as Earth's crust. With no possibility of earthquakes, Venus must have some way of releasing the pressure that would build up inside the core. Using the *Magellan* images, astronomers have identified some "hot spots" where volcanic activity may still be taking place. Astronomers assume these hot spots, then, are relieving the heat and pressure that is pushing up from deep inside the planet.

Lessons from Venus

The unique manner in which Venus vents its internal heat is just another aspect of the planet that clearly shows how different it is from Earth. Although the two planets were

Scientists suspect that there are still hot spots on Venus such as the Maat Mons volcano.

formed in the same region of space billions of years ago, they followed separate courses of evolution. Earth became a livable planet with many elements in balance that let life flourish. Venus, on the other hand, developed a thick atmosphere that caused the planet to suffer from the greenhouse effect, ensuring that nothing would ever live on its barren and dry surface.

Scientists are still very much interested in studying Venus precisely because they are unsure why its evolution was so different from that of its sister planet, Earth. By learning more about Venus, scientists hope to be able to answer many more questions about our own planet. For example, will the buildup of carbon dioxide from the burning of fossil fuels on Earth lead to the kind of greenhouse effect that makes Venus unlivable? Venus's atmosphere may hold the answer, and by examining it, scientists may be able to prevent such a disaster from ever occurring on Earth. In this way, Earth's twin might just hold a key to Earth's future.

Glossary

arachnoids: Patterns of ridges on Venus's surface that fan out like spiderwebs.

asteroid: A chunk of rock that orbits the sun like a planet. Asteroids vary greatly in size.

carbon dioxide: A gas that makes up a large portion of Venus's atmosphere.

comet: A heavenly body with a starlike center and a long, bright tail.

diameter: The distance across the center of a circle. Since planets are circular when viewed from any side, the diameter is in line with the planet's equator.

gravity: A force of attraction that draws all matter to the surface of the planet.

greenhouse effect: The dangerous buildup of heat around a planet.

orbit: The path of one heavenly body revolving around another.

pancake domes: Extinct, flat-topped volcanoes with steep sides. They received their name because they appear like pancakes in images taken by orbiting space probes.

retrograde motion: The spinning of a planet from east to west, which is opposite the direction most planets spin in the solar system.

spectroscopes: Scientific instruments that read light patterns from an object.

sulfuric acid: A substance found in Venus's cloud layers that eats away at anything it touches.

For Further Exploration

Duncan Brewer, *Venus*. New York: Marshall Cavendish, 1992. An excellent overview of the planet. The book is challenging but rewarding for young readers, and many fine photos and illustrations are placed throughout the text.

Patricia Lauber, *Journey to the Planets*. New York: Crown, 1993. An introductory guide to the planets and space exploration. From the landing on the moon to probes to other planets, this book covers what we know about heavenly bodies and how we know it.

The Near Planets. Alexandria, VA: Time-Life Books, 1989. An older but thorough study of Earth, Mars, Mercury, and Venus. The chapter on Venus discusses the many probes sent to Venus and the information they sent back.

This section also gives excellent detail on how the greenhouse effect operates on Venus. The book as a whole helps illustrate how the planets near the sun are related.

Gregory L. Vogt, *Venus*. Brookfield, CT: Millbrook Press, 1994. Part of the Gateway Solar System series, this introduction to the planet is perfect for young readers. Color and black-and-white photos and illustrations enhance the informative text.

Websites

NASA Kids. http://kids.msfc.nasa.gov. This is the space organization's website designed especially for kids. There is very basic information here on the planets and many fun projects to try. The site is updated regularly with reports on the best times to view astronomical events as well as upcoming NASA projects.

Welcome to the Planets. http://pds.jpl.nasa.gov/planets/welcome/venus.htm. A NASA-sponsored website devoted to images taken from various space probes sent throughout the solar system. A section on Venus has many good photos from *Magellan* and *Pioneer* missions.

Index